TIA MONIQUE

My Life As A #Girlboss

First published by Tia Monique 2022

Copyright © 2022 by Tia Monique

All rights reserved. No part of this publication may be reproduced, stored or transmitted in any form or by any means, electronic, mechanical, photocopying, recording, scanning, or otherwise without written permission from the publisher. It is illegal to copy this book, post it to a website, or distribute it by any other means without permission.

Tia Monique has no responsibility for the persistence or accuracy of URLs for external or third-party Internet Websites referred to in this publication and does not guarantee that any content on such Websites is, or will remain, accurate or appropriate.

Designations used by companies to distinguish their products are often claimed as trademarks. All brand names and product names used in this book and on its cover are trade names, service marks, trademarks and registered trademarks of their respective owners. The publishers and the book are not associated with any product or vendor mentioned in this book. None of the companies referenced within the book have endorsed the book.

First edition

This book was professionally typeset on Reedsy.
Find out more at reedsy.com

Contents

Acknowledgement	iv
Dr. Noreen Davis	1
Emily Motley-Wilson	4
Tameka Palmer	9
Tamara Brown	15
Melvina Pratt-Harris	19
Lillie Harris	23
Angelina Rideaux	25
Angelina Squire	30
Jana Devoe	39
Ena Friday	43
Princess Millens	48
About Our CoAuthors	53
Spotlight Authors	70
About the Author	76

Acknowledgement

I would like to thank every coauthor that made this project possible! Your stories about your journey in entrepreneurship is one of triumph and I am grateful to know each one of you!

It's my desire to continue to watch you grow and excel in your businesses. I can't wait to see you hit the 6 figure mark and beyond! I can't wait to see your names in lights all over the world! You all are extraordinary and outstanding girl bosses! It is your time!

With love,
   Your Coach and #1 supporter/pusher,
   Tia Monique

Dr. Noreen Davis

I NEVER KNEW!
CONCENTRATE ON GOING FORWARD

Proverbs 18:16 is a powerful statement that revealed my answer to my journey to entrepreneurship.

The word declared in the (NIV) "A gift opens the way and ushers the giver into the presence of the great" which the Lord revealed to me, was what I am designed to be known for, which was my gift.

God has put a talent in me for Inspirational teaching and empowering others to shift toward their spiritual destiny into the Kingdom and motivate them to keep moving forward. Never knew it was the gift that one day, the world will make or have room for, to put me in the presence of the great.

Before I knew the road I would be traveling as an inspirational speaker, I never knew it would also be a source of income, and I never would have ever dreamed of it. Thank You for every day I made choices that shape my life. It was God's wisdom as in Isaiah Chapter 11 verses 2-3. I prayed every day for years. I read Proverbs 18:16 for years, but never knew it could or would carry over to the marketplace to not just encourage and motivate the faith-based community. But the gift was also for the marketplace, which benefited corporate America and myself, how did it happen?

Someone asks me to tell my life story and I told them; raised in the suburbs of Long Island New York, my parents were government workers in the medical field, my mother and father were registered nurses, my sister, a social worker, and me -a corporate banker affirmative action EEO officer for a large bank for 12 years and then 20 years government work.

Most of us have some chapters you'd rather not share with anyone, but I ended up somewhere I never wanted to be (college days laughing out loud). I did things that cost me more than I ever thought I would have to pay for; I compromised values, and broke promises, but guess what? My story and your story weren't over. Regardless of what happened or what we have done or haven't done, your future is unwritten.

I never knew what entrepreneurship was, never thought about it, and wasn't around entrepreneurs. All I stood on was Proverbs 18 verse 16 which declares in NIV "A gift opens the way and ushers the giver into the presence of the great." On my journey, I started to ask myself, "What do I need to start doing to move in the direction of the life story I want to tell the world?"

Life as a B.O.S.S. became when God spoke clearly out of 2 Corinthians 5:17 (NIV) which declared to me "Therefore, if anyone is in Christ, the new creation has come: The old has gone, the new is here."

So on August 10, 2019, I got rebaptized in Detroit MI Camp Meeting (Get my church to Pentecost) by Bishop Corletta J. Vaughn. All things became new thereafter, and the Holy Spirit not only changed my mindset but also changed the way I worked my business.

My business changed in such a way that God enlarged my territory with my platform, by training and developing passionate, God-seeking disciple-making believers of Christ who were and still are infused with the person and power of the Holy Spirit in all that they do. He showed me, even in the marketplace, how to empower, encourage and influence those who have ears to hear the sound of Kingdom without them realizing I was the light with standards in business and I made the difference wherever my foot trod. (God ordered my steps in Business).

Now, I know that if you keep God first in all you do, all other good things will be added to you.

If you don't know, just concentrate on going forward with God in front of you and your business.

Remember, Isaiah 11:2-3 declares "The Spirit of the Lord will rest on him- The Spirit of wisdom and understanding, The Spirit of counsel and of might, The Spirit of the knowledge and fear of the Lord- and he will delight in the fear of the Lord."

Keep Moving and Stay Focused
Rev. Dr. Noreen Davis
Spiritual Influencer

Emily Motley-Wilson

Do All that He Calls You to Do!

Hey, you there! Yes, you! Have you ever wanted to do something that would change the lives of not just you, but so many other people? If that's you, then this is for you.

Being an entrepreneur was never anything I considered an option. I'm not really sure why it wasn't, as my father was a business owner, eventually. I guess it was mostly because our parents instilled in us to school, get a good education, and then be able to get a good paying job.

The funny thing is, God blessed my father to have his own business after working so many years for someone else. So why didn't this event cross my mind to venture out to do the same? Why was I blank concerning entrepreneurship? It's a great question. The truth is, I never even entertained the thought. So, like the word says, as a man thinketh, so is he. I thought a good job was the way, and that was the extent to which my mind could conceive at the time. This is exactly why you can't trust your own mind in its natural state. It must be trained and exposed to where you're predestined to go.

In 1998, my journey began as an entrepreneur, when I entered into what we call the "Pink Bubble" world in Mary Kay, as an Independent Beauty Consultant. My friend needed someone to join her team, and I was definitely going to help her in any way that I could. I had one goal in mind but had no thought of how I could achieve it. I went to meetings religiously. I needed to recruit three people to achieve my ultimate goal – to become a Red Jacket. The way they were celebrated when they marched into each meeting, the recognition, and the prestige. I would watch others and how they interacted with them. I made many facial bookings, color make-up sessions with some of the kindest women, but no one, NOT ONE person ever signed up with me during my year and a half run in Mary Kay.

By now, my life was getting pretty busy. As a wife, a mother of three, and the choir director, I sang on the praise team, served on the prayer ministry, the outreach ministry, and oversaw the children's church ministry; all while holding down (9-5) - my hands were full. So, I had to let Mary Kay go. I went years without running a business because I just couldn't see where I could fit it into my busy schedule. However, there was still something inside of me yearning to be a business owner.

Fast forward a few years. Around 2010, I joined 5-Linx with some more friends who are truly like my blood family. While in this business, the Lord allowed me to serve as my friend's assistant. This opened my eyes to business on a whole new level. It also afforded me the opportunity to handle hundreds of thousands of dollars.

During my time within this business, I learned how business relationships foster the opening of other doors when your character and integrity are married. If you want to know what keeps you a real boss, it's having integrity when no one is looking. I can't tell you how many times I had someone else's money, and I mean BIG money, in my hands and care. I always treated it like I would want someone to handle my own money. Due to health issues, I had to shut down a business that brought me lots of joy, fun and success.

Being in the room with Vice Presidents and Executives within this company, gave me a glimpse of things to come. He was preparing me for where I was going, not for where I was. Once again, the entrepreneur in me had been put on hold. I was prospering on my 9-5, but something was still missing.

Serving in church, my family, and working my job kept me pretty busy; but I knew there was something more I needed to do. While riding with my sister-friend to lunch after church one Sunday, I shared with her my desire to start a business in the event planning space. I further shared how my oldest sister, Narcissa and I had planned to open a wedding business, where we would offer catering and decorating. Ingrid and I had completed several successful events; where she did the coordinating, and I did the decorating. We had never charged a dime for any of these events. On the ride to eat lunch that day, Majestic Creations Wedding & Event Planning was birthed in 2019.

Yes! My joy was back! We immediately got our first wedding through being willing & obedient to the Lord telling us to help a bride that was a bit overwhelmed due to little help. We went to work! The Lord did what He does! Oh, did I mention that we had 2 weeks to pull this wedding for 200 guests off? Oh, OK! Being a girl boss also requires sacrifice, patience, and compassion. My God! They are a must! Out of this one wedding, Majestic Creations received some exposure, and we booked our next wedding. This is why you have to trust what you hear and not how you feel or how people can make you feel.

My business partner and I were super excited. We were on our way. We knew we had to invest in branding ourselves if we were going to attract the customers that we were looking for. So, we did just that. We hired a phenomenal company that crafted our website, business cards, flyers, set up all of our social media platforms, etc. You couldn't tell anything; we were official!

We invested a bit more and attended a Bridal Expo. You are talking about work!!! Oh, this was a lot of work, but our booth was beautiful! We had hundreds of brides come by our booth, talk with us and leave their information. We had positioned ourselves, and we were headed in the right direction. We were booking appointments left and right, to the point that Ingrid and I had to keep each other straight on which couple we were meeting.

It was such a joy talking with couples, hearing their thoughts, helping them with things they'd never thought about, and offering solutions to all of those things. The business was flourishing, and then it happened; the pandemic hit in 2020! Initially, we didn't feel it as much, but then just as you thought, people postponed their weddings or decided to go a different route altogether.
So, yes…the business was on hold AGAIN!

Meanwhile, I had been looking for a Mary Kay consultant, because mine had passed away. Unfortunately, no one I asked knew of one. So, one day, my husband and I went to try a new restaurant in Burlington, NC. While in there, guess who I saw? A Mary Kay lady who had a table set up. She was trying to get my name and number, and my husband was pulling me away from the table, saying "Come on!"

Well, I was able to leave my name and number. She called me to set up a facial and she asked me to come back to Mary Kay. I wanted to say no, but the Lord whispered to me, "Sometimes you have to become the resolution to your own problem." So, that night, I became a Mary Kay consultant for the second time.

I signed up in November of 2020, submitted for DIQ (Director in Qualification) in January 2021, and officially became an Independent Sales Director on 1 February 2021 (although I technically finished in 29 days). Only the Lord could do this! I've earned three career cars since being in Mary Kay. My first car (the Malibu) was earned as a Consultant in January 2021, and the second two, the Equinox and the Camaro were earned in June 2021.

Being a girl boss will require us to make time for the things that God said we should do.

Along this entrepreneur road, my leadership skills have been strengthened, my integrity has grown, even more, my people skills have been enhanced, my core principles have been made surer and I've never been more firm on the thought that, whatever the Lord says you can do, you definitely can do it.

The road may not be easy, and the plans that you make may not be what actually happens; but know this, anything that's too easy, probably was not the best road for you to travel, and if we never put a plan in place, we don't have a roadmap to where we're going.

I believe there is a season for everything, and God has a plan. While it is to prosper us, and not hurt us, it was never promised everything within a season will be pleasant. Take courage, and know that all things work together for good to them that love God, to them who are the called according to His purpose. I feel a changing of the Guards! What will the next season bring? Stay tuned...

Tameka Palmer

QUICK question...Have you ever beaten the odds?

Being raised by a single, black woman, on government assistance, while living in subsidized housing was common in my community.

I didn't feel poor. We (my mom, older brother, and I) never missed a meal. We never had our lights or gas disconnected. We had a clean, roach-free, nicely decorated apt.

I, because of child support, always had the latest fashionable clothes and shoes. I started going to a professional hair stylist at the young age of 5. I had long, extra thick hair that my mom said she ain't about to wrestle with every day. Lol, my birthdays were joyous and my Christmas lists were checked off from top to bottom.

But, according to the statistics, we lacked sufficient amount of income to live at a standard that is considered comfortable or normal in society.

We were poor!

The fact that I am being featured alongside a fantastic group of other girl bosses in this anthology is mind-blowing to me.

How did I get here?

Because, according to the statistics, I am not supposed to be a girl boss.

According to the statistics, I was not supposed to break the financial, generational curse on my life, go to school to be a nurse, and move my momma up out of the same three-bedroom apt that I had spent 14 years of my childhood in. But, I did!

Again, I ask myself...how did I get here?

I was always placed in leadership roles and trainings in school as well as for all of my former employees. I never understood why. In my eyes, I didn't display any signs that I was a leader. I had a bubbly personality and I talked a lot. I also talk fast, which in turn made me stumble through and mispronounce some of my words.

As a matter of fact, I have a secret about my communication skills. I was placed in speech therapy classes in elementary school. They quickly found out that that was a mistake when I started helping the therapist teach the other kids in our sessions. Lol

After I graduated high school, I fell in love with an older guy. We had a toxic relationship. He was physically, emotionally, mentally, and psychologically abusive. I was paralyzed by fear throughout the relationship. It had gotten to the point of he was going to kill me or I was going to have to kill him to protect my own life.
I made up my mind to take my chances on leaving. I mean I was in a lose-lose situation either way. After eight years, I got the courage to leave. Not knowing what I know now about Domestic Violence and because I hadn't researched narcissism, I thought he'd changed. I got back with him after a

four-year split. All to get back into a relationship all over again with Dr. Jekyll and Mr. Hyde. The second go-round lasted four years.

Throughout the relationship, I questioned Yah "WHY?" Why me? Was I that bad of a person that I deserved to be treated so horribly?

After getting out of that deadly relationship, I went to school to be a nurse. Taking care of people was my happy place. My bubbly personality and hilarious sense of humor made my rapport with my patients unique. I always had a special place in their hearts. They would immediately start to treat me like family.

After several years of nursing, I started feeling unfulfilled. My daily prayer to Yah was for Him to tell me my purpose. Was nursing not it?

I began to talk about my abusive relationship…little by little. It was suggested I talk to a Coach by the name of Tia Monique. We immediately had a divine connection and she suggested I start a non-profit for Domestic Violence.

In 2016, Pearls of Resilience, Inc. was born. We are an advocacy foundation for women and children affected by Domestic Violence. I became an Awareness Advocate. I started spreading awareness and was invited to speak at numerous community events throughout the southeast.

In 2017, I opened Meaningful Merchandise Thrift Shoppe. MMTS was used as a catalyst to provide funding for Pearls of Resilience, Inc.

In 2017, I also connected with the Georgia Coalition Against Domestic Violence. I joined their Community Rise Program. I became one of their guest panelists for various events. One of the most epic events for me was when I was a panelist at our State Capitol. GCADV also invited me to be their official speaker for their Frontline Training for New Advocates. I have a segment where I share my testimony and allow the attendees to ask questions afterwards.

In 2019, I was accepted into LEAP Academy (Leadership Education and Advancement for Professionals. LEAP's primary purpose is to enhance the professional skills of individuals of color; seeking professional advancement in the anti-violence against women field.

The same person that never saw herself as a leader, the same person that always doubted her abilities, the same person that overcame and healed from Domestic Violence, the same person that, according to statistics, was not supposed to be on the journey that her life was on….was chosen to be a part of a national Cohort with a spectacular group of leaders, ranging from the east coast to west coast.

In 2019, the Holy Spirit spoke to me. I was asleep and I heard the phrase "Life Coach." I am certain it was the Holy Spirit because it was crystal clear and it awakened me out of my sleep.

At that time, I hadn't ever heard of Life Coaching. I immediately started researching the business and well-known Life Coaches.

Soon thereafter, I became a Certified Life Coach and started G.L.O Girl Coaching Society.

I jumped out there with no net and I sank! I didn't have a strategy, plan, or a Coach of my own. My confidence was shattered and my self-doubt was at an all-time high. My inner critic was downing me in both ears.

I questioned the whole life coach venture.

YAH immediately reminded me with confirmation, "YES" I heard him correctly and to not give up!

He also reminded me of my WHY:

- To live a life of freedom without any financial restrictions for me.
- To impact those women's lives that need help with loving themselves after heartbreak.

The same way he graciously helped me to do it. I did not experience all that heartache from Domestic Violence in vain.

He restored me mentally, emotionally, and spiritually.

"And no one pours new wine into old wineskins. Otherwise, the wine will burst the skins, and both the wine and the wineskins will be ruined. No, they pour new wine into new wineskins." - Mark 2:22

I decided to pursue my passion again.

This time, YAH blessed me with a fantastic group of Coaches that believed in me when I had stopped believing in myself.

Now, I have a plan and strategy.

I bounced back!

I'm currently a Freedom and Self-Care Coach. I show women who have experienced past hurt, how to obtain freedom through self-care and self-love.

I am the admin of Healthy Relationship Headquarters for Women on Facebook. This is a private, safe-space community for like-minded women to explore their lived experiences related to relationships, self-love, self-care, healing, and boundaries.

My girl boss journey has been rocky. It has had uncertainties, surprises, teachable moments, and small and big wins.

I'm still trusting the process because of YAH's promises.

After all, according to the statistics, I was never expected to level up and be on this journey as a girl boss!

Tamara Brown

Negativity, doubt, fear, despair, disappointment, resentment, feeling inferior, feeling not enough, and feeling unworthy were all the emotions I felt whenever the thought came to my mind about starting my business.

As a child, no one planted a seed that one day I could be my own boss and become a female entrepreneur. Instead, I was encouraged to go to college and become the first one in my immediate family to graduate and get a degree. I succeeded in accomplishing that goal but I felt in my heart that God had something more for me.

As a little girl, I read daily with aspirations that one day, I would become an Author. It seemed like a far fetched dream that would never become a reality as I started and stopped writing many times. I knew that's what I needed to be doing as God continued to download titles after titles in me even in my sleep.

I continued to work my full-time job day in and day out supporting others as they wrote books, sold jewelry, dinners, cakes, candles etc. Many ideas and visions came that I either talked myself out of or let someone else talk me out of doing what I know God had given me to do. However, I, one day realized that these emotions and people were blocking me and keeping me from becoming the Prosperous Woman that God intended for me to be.

I took a leap of faith as God connected me and equipped me with what I needed to become an entrepreneur. My journey started as a girl boss when I was introduced to an online wellness shopping club by a dear friend of mine. It was something that I prayed about many times and did not know how or where to begin. It all happened after prayer.

My youngest son started having trouble with his breathing and had to be taken to the emergency room at least three times in 2018. They were indeed the scariest times in our lives. He was eventually referred to a Respiratory Therapist and was diagnosed with asthma and further testing was done to determine that he was allergic to dust as well as cockroaches. I was asked what I was using to clean my home and then informed that the chemicals could be causing my son's asthma flare-ups. Consequently, it was recommended that I use products without harsh chemicals.

It was at that time that I came across another Girl Boss that was sharing an online wellness shopping club with the non-toxic cleaning products. It was exactly what I prayed for and needed at the time. I tried the products and loved them. My son's breathing began to get better and we had no more trips to the emergency room.

When I was asked about building my own business, I was hesitant at first but realized that this online shopping club was the answer to my prayers and it could be the answer to another mother's prayer. I started inviting other ladies to join me. I began helping mothers and families make the switch to products that are safer for their homes and their families. It was something that I was passionate about doing.

Fear would creep in every time I thought about leaving my job. Then one day while I was working from home, I unexpectedly received a telephone call from my Supervisor and Human Resources informing me that I was being permanently laid off due to Covid. After 6 years and at the age of 46, I had never lost a job. I had worked since I was 15 years old. I was devastated as I thought my job was secure but little did I know at the time that it wasn't.

I learned a valuable lesson through all of that and that is to always have a plan B no matter how secure you think you are on your job. These companies can fire you and let you go at any time without any given reason. All of the time, I wanted to give up on my business and not share it with others. I'm so glad I didn't. That day God closed the door I was too afraid to walk away from on my own and opened new doors for me to do what I was purposed to do.

Not having a full-time job anymore afforded me the time to focus on enhancing the lives of women by helping them achieve their goals and build their own businesses. I had more time to spend with my family and create beautiful memories.

I Co-Authored my first book titled, "Testaments Of Survivors Women Healed and Whole"with some amazing Women of God published through a remarkable Publishing Company, Let It Out Academy. Since then, I've Co-Authored two additional books, "The Fervent Prayers Of A Mother and "Making Moves Not Excuses." I'm currently working on my 5th book "Be Free From Obesity," a 90-day planner to help those who are struggling to overcome obesity. I am also writing this chapter for "My Life As a Girl Boss." This is my 6th assignment and to God alone be all the Glory!

My Life As Girl Boss has not been an easy journey. There have been many days I wanted to give up but my God wouldn't allow me to quit. There were days I put my all into my business. There were days when life happened and I didn't work my business at all. Thinking every day would be easy, I was WRONG. ☐

Here's the thing…life started, and I fell off track many times. I don't care how long you've been in business; life can hit you hard at times. When the alarm clock goes off at 5am, don't hit snooze. When watching TV seems better than working, make the right choice. When hanging with friends seems fun but your coins aren't together, be smart. When you have a business idea that you've done nothing with: plan some time to work on your biz

When everyone is relying on you but you've reached your limits, say no. Sounds easy, right? It's not. This is why we have to show up and do the work consistently. Consistency + Discipline = RESULTS

With discipline, we can achieve anything we desire personally & professionally. I can say that I owe my success today to God and to being disciplined. To all the Girl Bosses or ladies reading this who have a desire to be an entrepreneur and have not yet started, just START.
"Launch the business now and perfect it later," were the words I heard loud and clear when God gave me the vision to start. "Simply Mr. and Mrs. Thrifty. When I listened to God and launched my business, He sent people with large donations to me without me asking. God told me to start with what I had and that's exactly what I did. I've learned to move when God says move. If you wait and hesitate, before you know it, someone will be doing what God had given you to do because it has to be perfect.

Don't allow perfectionism to keep you from your dream of starting a business. If you continue to wait for the perfect time to start, it will never come as you will continue to find faults and reasons not to get started. Be encouraged and know that quitting is not an option! Giving up is not an option! Walking away is not an option!

Be strong, vigorous and courageous Girl Bosses! Complete the assignment that God has destined for you to do and walk in the purpose that He has divinely ordered just for you. This is your time and your season! Our God has not given us the spirit of fear so we must send fear back to where it came! From this day forward, we will no longer walk in fear! We will walk in FAITH! We will make moves, not excuses! Much love and KINGDOM blessings to you all BOSS GIRLS!!

Melvina Pratt-Harris

My Journey As A Girl Boss

I want to say that I was motivated in 2001 or should I say bitten by the entrepreneurial bug. I am reminded that it has been with me since I was a kid with candy and lemonade stands during the sizzling summer months. Some might say, I have always been one to take that risk or step out on faith even before I realized what that all meant. My mind says that 2001 would be the time in my life when I had to learn to stand alone and take that step. I worked full time at age 33 for a young lady, 10 years younger than me. She owned a cell phone shop in which I worked daily from 9:00 AM to 6:00 PM. No break, no lunch. This seemed quite unfair as I was not accustomed to working straight through all those hours every week. I soon learned that in Georgia, there was no law stating otherwise. Yeah, OK, this is not going to work for me. But as for a young boss, it worked well for her. I eventually quit and made a mental note that if she at age 23, could be her own boss, so could I. Why Not Me?

In 2001, during the winter months, I decided that I was tired of the 12-hour shifts which I had been working at the hospital since leaving the cell phone store. I decided that winter that I was going to step out on faith (Hebrews 11:1, Now faith is the assurance of things hoped for, the conviction of things not seen) and be my own boss. I asked my husband if it would it be okay if I open a home daycare. I promised him that if I could not make this work within a year, I would go back to work, and he agreed.

December 2001, I opened Harris Family Daycare. An in-home childcare service for six or less children. That daycare lasted till 2005, renamed Kidventures Childcare in 2003. That was my first time stepping out as my own boss, and for four years, it was very lucrative for me. I was Awarded Home of Distinction in 2005 and received my National Administrators Credentials. This would be my first bona fide experience as a girl boss.

After closing the daycare in 2005, I moved to Michigan. I was going to do daycare in Michigan, but the rules in Georgia were different from the rules in Michigan. Moreover, I needed more schooling, which I did not have time to get because I needed to get a job so I could take care of my family. I have had other times that I would attempt to do business, but nothing ever really happened.

I would not take that leap again until June of 2014. I decided again that I wanted to be my own boss. I was tired of working for other people. I quit my job making good money to again pursue my dream to start another business. Moving back to Georgia trying to decide what I wanted to do, my business venture would be Personal Concierge known as In the Nik of Time.

Before I start any business, I tried to do my research. I got the training I needed to start this business. I started in the fall of 2014, setting up a legal LLC, Pharris Vision Enterprises LLC setting up my business properly. I did not know back in 2005 that I was operating illegally. Growth is a wonderful thing. So here I am in 2014, I started as a Personal Concierge business. It did not work out for me; I was hurt because I shared too much information thinking I was amongst people who I thought had my best interest at heart. I would soon come to find out that they were taking mental notes, and the next thing I know, they were Personal Concierges as well.

Not thinking that it is enough room for us all to do business in this industry together, (What God has for you no person can take away) but because they took what I had planned as their own, it really hurt me. I hurt so bad that I decided to take off in another direction and I opened the home call center. I worked for myself as a Call Center agent for about a year and a half until I got tired of being confined to the house. I dropped the business again, not to pick it up again until 2016. I would go back into business again; this time as a Virtual Assistant. That worked out well for me. I got my business as a Virtual Assistant and reopened the Call Center as well.

Again, I let myself get into my head. Fear came over me heavily. I was afraid of success and procrastination set in. As a result, everything fell apart in 2017. I know that I am my own worst enemy; I talked myself out of a lot of great opportunities; I self-sabotaged myself. I must be honest about that. Nobody helped me talk myself out of it. I am afraid of the unknown. What am I afraid of? Why am I afraid? I wonder if I did everything that I needed to do with my business. What would it really look like? So, I dropped it all in 2017. I went back to work Summer of 2017.

I worked jobs that were not the best paying and I had to answer to someone else. I did not like it, but I needed to do something. I did work a side business in Jewelry, BE Visual Jewelry as an Independent Paparazzi Consultant which I still have today. Paparazzi has produced some extraordinarily Successful Consultants. If you work the Business, it will work for you. As for myself, I can tell my truth. Today, it is more a hobby than a business as I am not the girly girl I thought I wanted to be. I am just a T-shirt and blue jeans kind of girl with my everyday silver or gold hoop earrings. I do not dress up daily and I only wear costume jewelry on occasion. I do not like to go LIVE; I love to do vendor events when the opportunity presents itself. So I cannot say that I have given this business 100 % of my time but I have not given up either. I love the jewelry; I really do. I am just not that salesperson type.

I continued to work through March of 2021 minus the break of the Pandemic which lasted about 6 months. I went back to work in September 2021 but that did not last. I worked a job for hours I hated and did not feel like I was being respected as an employee much less a senior to my co-worker. I decided again to take that leap of faith and say, Lord, I am just going to go for it. I left the airport. I am forever grateful to God who never gives up on Me. May 2021, I decided that this time, I would take that leap again and never look back. I have not returned to work for anybody since I left the airport in 2021. I just celebrated 1 year of Independence in May 2022. I have successfully launched a second business as Freight Dispatcher. God is on my side; my launch date was scheduled for June 1, 2022, and I was blessed with an Owner Carrier with 3 trucks on May 31, 2022. Isn't God good? TGBTG! Keep On Moving! With Christ all things are possible. Just take Him at His word. These things were manifested in my vision board 2022.

Lillie Harris

Hello!
My name is Lillie Harris, and this is a little bit of my business story and the ups and downs with it. All of my life, all I know is work. I've been working since I was 11 years old. My father always taught me that if you want something, you go work for it. So I have been what they call a go-getter ever since.
I've done everything from being a bingo caller to working in a nursing home, to working in a warehouse, but mostly in the restaurant field where I'm ServSafe and highly qualified. I am currently a full-time caregiver to my mother who has advanced dementia, but before that, I did still work full-time.

Life hasn't been all sunshine; I am a recovering addict, but I know too that God won't put any more on us than we can bear and He can bring us out of all things. In August 2021, my mom tested positive for Covid-19 which further advanced her dementia, so I quit my job and began taking care of my her and have been doing so ever since. At one point, I got behind in my bills and was referred to a program that helps with financial assistance. I spoke with a lady named Mrs. Joyner who would become my case manager, and later my supposedly coach. I poured my heart out to her.
On October 7th, 2021, I met with Mrs. Joyner face to face; she presented me with a business opportunity. I talked it over with my husband and he told

me to go for it, so I jumped out on faith and that's what I did. Once I joined Herbalife, there were a lot of times I just wanted to give up. The person who introduced me to the business and was supposed to be my coach just left me hanging, so I had to learn it all on my own and I did and did it my way! I drove all the way to Minnesota to get the training and tools that I would need to be successful in this business. I solely work on social media because my mother comes first, and it fits better with my schedule.

I also run a second business which is an online wellness shopping club. I started this online shopping club on April 3rd, 2022. The purpose is to get people to replace all of their household products such as Clorox, washing powder, bar soap, etc. With 100% plant-based non-toxic products and having them shipped directly to your doorstep, you spend only what you can afford. I chose this business because I thought of myself and how I was at one time. I had no transportation, no way to get household supplies, etc. So that's where the online shopping club came into play because I thought about those less fortunate, the elderly, and those without transportation.

I'm all about helping people and wanting what's best for them. For most of my life, I've been afraid to speak up for myself. That was until I met two beautiful ladies who became my coaches and have helped me further get where I am right now; Ms. Tashauna Richardson and Mrs. Tia Monique. I thank God every day for these two wonderful ladies. For pushing me, for answering questions whenever I ask, and so much more. These ladies are truly amazing! Lillie Harris knows that it is far from complete, but just beginning.

Angelina Rideaux

Life As A Girl Boss

See, I never really saw myself as a boss. I didn't think that I could own my business or even become an author. Since the age of 15, I was engaged in fast food. It's crazy how God works. God knows our next step, even when we don't know. I was afraid to step into the world. I was afraid of the life God promised me. Growing up, I was told you must finish high school and go to college to get a good job. No one taught me or showed me how to become an entrepreneur.

As kids, we dream about becoming lawyers, chefs, teachers, police officers and so on. Who teaches us to turn those dreams into becoming our own bosses? All these years growing up, I thought you had to have a college degree to be successful. I just learned that there are people who didn't even have a college degree or even a high school diploma and they are very successful. I encourage you to read Think and Grow Rich by Napoleon Hill.

I spent years in college trying to figure out who I am and what I wanted in life. I changed my major a few times. I even stopped going to, for a while because I needed to work. To provide for my children, I found myself lost and confused for a long time. I felt like I had no chance in life. I knew that this wasn't the life I wanted to live, but for some reason, I was trapped in my own head. I believed that I wasn't educated enough to even think I could have my own business.

A few years ago, my therapist told me I should write a book. I laughed to myself. I couldn't afford to write a book. At the time, I was dealing with a lot. So, there was no way to believe I could do it. We don't realize that we are our own worst enemy. Because I believed that I couldn't do it, I didn't. I allowed my fears and self-doubt to get the best of me. I was allowing the devil to pick and choose which direction. I should go.

Being a girl boss doesn't happen overnight. Sometimes we don't even think about becoming a boss. Growing up, I didn't know anyone who owned their own business, nor did anyone teach us about owning our own business. It was all about going to school so you can get a good job.

2019 is when it all began for me. I lost my job of seven years. I worked for McDonald's; I started as a crew member and worked my way up to become a general manager. I was determined to make a career out of it, but God had other plans. I was arrested for theft and lost my job. I became depressed. Every day I had to talk myself out of killing myself. There were days that I didn't want to get out of bed. I could not believe that this was happening to me. I was scared and afraid of what was about to happen in my life. I was the sole provider for my family. How was I going to get another job? I didn't have a clue how I was going to get through this. I slept most of the day, so I wouldn't have to think about what was happening in my life.

With me crying every day, and being depressed, I forgot about my family, my kids, and my husband even when they still needed me. I had to find a way to move forward regardless. My husband, Dad and Mom were great supporters; they tried their best to keep me focused. But I needed something else. They couldn't help me. I had to help myself first. I had to find my own way out.

One morning, I woke up and went to Facebook. I saw that I had an invite from my best friend, Amanda Ashford to join a Facebook group called I Am

Beautiful The Movement. I accepted the request. When I went to the group, I saw all these amazing, phenomenal women telling their stories. One story really grabbed my attention because I could relate. Even though our story wasn't the same, I still could relate. I ended up buying her book, The Nine Lines by Tashauna Richardson. She's the founder of this group. After I read her story, right then, I knew I could do it. I knew that I had a story that I needed to tell. It was time for me to tell my truth. I said to Myself, "Here are women who have walked through fire and they are not afraid to speak out, not afraid to go for what they believe. So why haven't I made the move yet?"

I believed that I could do it. I saw that it could be done. God told me it was time. What was stopping me? Fear of rejection and failure was the cause of my standstill. I didn't want to put myself through another storm. I was afraid. Not only that, I didn't want to put my husband in any kind of bind. I had put our family through enough. He was our money maker, and I knew that writing a book costs money; money we just didn't have at that moment. We have six kids that we must provide for, bills that needed to be paid, and to top it off, I'm on probation and must pay over $25,000 dollars. So, there was no way I could even think about writing a book or even starting a business. In my head, I was thinking how is it time. I found myself questioning God again.

I had to realize three things: 1. I needed to build a relationship with God. I had to find my way back to Him. I had to quit blaming Him for everything bad that was happening in my life. I had to understand His way of doing things. 2. I had to step into faith. I couldn't be afraid anymore. I had to believe in myself. 3. I had to forgive myself and others. I had to start loving myself.

You might think that these three things are easy; in reality, they're not. There are a lot of women who can't get past number one. I know because it took me years to turn my life back over to God. Once I started building my relationship with God, He started to make moves in my life. He gave me the strength to talk to my husband about work, and about writing my first book. My husband didn't hesitate to say yes. So right then, I reached out to the founder of I AM Beautiful, The Movement, Tashauna Richardson to see how I can start writing the book. She sent me her publisher's name. I messaged her and from there, I was beginning to tell my truth.

Not only was I starting to write my book, God had blessed us with the COVID-19 stimulus funds, which me and my husband invested into starting our own loan service. J.O.T Unlimited Enterprises LLC. Now I am an author, inspirational speaker as well co-owner of J.O.T Unlimited Enterprises LLC.

My first book is, 'My Truth, No More Secrets,' it's on Amazon. It's a memoir about my life growing up. I created my first planner Lady Blue Jay Holding Our Sisters Accountable. It's on Amazon as well. I created this planner to help our sisters accomplish the goals they want to complete in life.

Having the courage to step into faith takes a lot of self-motivation. That's why you need to have a relationship with God. I knew that to continue to move in His name, I was going to have to clean up my surroundings. I was going to have to change something in my life. There were things that I was going to have to sacrifice to find my purpose in life. My life took a different direction, all because of an invitation to a group, 'I Am Beautiful The Movement.'

See, when you think you can't do it, there are women who think you can. We must go out into the world and not be afraid to show the world who we are. Even though my life as a girl boss started off rocky, the journey has been a blessing. I always say there is a reason for everything that happened in a person's life. God is showing us our purpose in life. He is showing us what he created us for.

By me losing my job, being arrested and becoming a felon, I thought my life was over. I thought God didn't love me at all. I wanted to give up and die. By Grace of His love, my Father God was not giving up on me. He knew my purpose in life. He needed me to see that. See God shows us signs, the signs that we asked for. I refuse to see those signs. So, he had to show me in a way that I would understand.

My last words to you as a girl boss are; don't be afraid of failure or rejection. Use your fears as motivation to get to your destination. Know that you are worthy, know that you are loved. You can do whatever you put your mind to. Know that giving up is not an option. There is someone who needs to hear your story.

Follow these three things to start your life as a girl boss. 1. Build a relationship with God. 2. Step into faith. And 3. Self-love.

People would ask, "Who are you?" Like most, I would say a mother, wife or now an author, inspirational speaker, etc. But if you would ask me that question now. Who are you? My response would be. I'm a child of God. I'm a survivor. I'm a woman of faith. I'm a woman of courage and strength. I'm a woman of change.

Angelina Squire

When Special Need Parenting Build Girl Bosses For Entrepreneurship

Running any business on your own takes a lot of commitment, courage and I must add sacrifices. Being a parent can be a challenging enough job on its own. Now add special need parenting, and caregiver into the equation and this becomes multiple jobs within one. I know because I am a Girl Boss Mompreneur, raising a son that is living on the Autism spectrum. Autism spectrum disorder refers to a broad range of conditions characterized by challenges with social skills, repetitive behaviors, speech and nonverbal communication.

Mounting difficulties can become overwhelming for special needs parents, because we experience unique challenges every single day. Feelings of overwhelm is one factor why manyfind themselves, quitting before even beginning to embark on the journey of entrepreneurship.Not only did becoming a Girl Boss Mompreneur gave me freedom to chase my passions, it also drove me to find the time to support and be present with my Autistic son.

Six of the top questions, I'm often asked about being a Girl Boss Mompreneur, and a special need parent:

1. How did I start a Health and wellness business?

2.How did I coach myself to lose sixty-four pounds as a result of launching my health and wellness business?

3.How did I build a 501 (c) 3 Nonprofit for Autism/various disabilities families without grants, and living on low income?

4.How did I build an LLC, teaching clients how to regain control of their mind, body, and soul?

5. Where do I find the time to coach- mentor others, and run a care giver support group?

6. How do I balance it all while parenting my special need son, a wife and a mother to my two other children, all while I'm on disability, and still remain sane?

I first had to become aware that, I'm not the only one facing challenges. Secondly, I had to understand that no one is exempt from facing challenges in life. One of my philosophies, I live by that allows me to run, build my businesses and adequately take care of my family in the face of life challenges is; "Challenges does not mean impossible!

The two Faces of Fear

Fear can paralyze you or it can become a personal navigation system that direct you towards a more meaningful life, re-routing you during difficult times. One of my favorite quotes I created, and teach is; Fear is a self-made prison that we choose to allow our mindset to become caged within. There will always be fear. It's your daily decision of choosing which face of fear, you're going to live by.

How you use fear, will determine if you will find the points of joy while traveling through life's challenges. Paralyzing fear, or the inner/outer re-routing navigation of fear, both can become drivers in one's life. Which one are you choosing today? I needed something more in my life than what a regular nine to five could give me for my family.

Like many parents, I became trapped within the comfort of my job with the mindset that believed I was only capable of working within the medical field, with the skill set I thought I only had. I wanted a life I could live on my own terms, create my own schedule- no longer being told when and how much time I could be present with my family. When I first stepped into the lane of entrepreneurship, fear paralyzed me and I gave up many times because of fear of failure.

Thoughts of, what if it doesn't work haunted me. I didn't want to proceed forward because of the nagging thoughts; what if I failed, what if I let my family down and become the laughing stock of the world? I struggled with inner fears that my son's behaviors, his ongoing needs for one-on-one care, numerous doctor visits, my insecurities, feeling not educated enough, and believing my life was excessively full- and to hectic to build or create anything that can add value to the world.

Entrepreneurship seemed so impossible for me. I can recall the conversations, inner dialogue Ihad with myself. Repeated conversations; I would never be capable of starting a businessbecause of reoccurring thoughts that special needs parents will only have the life that their child's disabilities create for them. This kind of thinking blocks any positive, forward momentum in your personal and professional life.

I became depressed and hopeless as I continued to work my nine to five. My fears becamestronger than my desire to go after the time freedom I desired to have. I continued working my nine to five, contributing to fulfilling someone else's dreams, their visions as I continued to suffer as a dreamer. You are aware that you are a machine, pushing someone else's dream as you continuously punch into someone else's time clock, right? This happens when you neglect toactively clock into your own life, and utilize that nine to five to help fund and build your own dreams and life's purpose.

Yes, we all need income to support ourselves and our families; the misconception comes into play when we believe that a nine to five is the only source of income.

Looking at the lives of special need parenting/caregivers you may miss the amazingentrepreneur characteristics, these parents and caregivers have as a result of their unexpected journey with their child with special needs.

Three characteristics an entrepreneur has in common with Special need parenting Girl Bosses.

1.Problem-solving- Problem-solving is no doubt one of the most important aspects of entrepreneurship. The essence of every business, is looking for problems to solve. Entrepreneurs are problem solvers who offers solutions, and getting them to the right people.

Special need parenting Girl Bosses, not only have skills in problem solving, they develop unique strategies with problem solving, because they think outside of the box. These Boss Moms are often presented with challenges, problems that drives them to becoming mass creators in solving their child's problems. This gives them an edge to effortlessly solve problems within their businesses. This edge is highly needed because problems are not absent for building or maintaining any businesses.

2. Self-leadership- Not everyone is born with a rush, a drive to change the world. Some believe, the life they can only have, is only the life they see that's challenged and distorted by images of their hardships. Looking at one of the various personality's traits of a successful entrepreneur, work ethics are among their success tools. Successful entrepreneurs work ethics are not basic level action.

Basic level action does the bare minimum, are comfortable with going wherever the chips may fall. When the going gets tough, basic level entrepreneurs show up in their business late, work less hours as they burn away more time on non-income producing activities. Special need parenting, Girl Boss entrepreneurs, are no strangers to the grind of the superior actions of a successful entrepreneur. The daily routine of caring for their special need child, the demands of their care has groomed them to wake up early when most people just sleep in.

They tackle the care of their children needs, life, their top priorities regardless if it's the weekend, holidays or work. They do what's necessary until the job is complete, just like successful entrepreneurs with vigorous work ethnics. Entrepreneurship has the ability of creatingmassive opportunities to learn, and grow you into a master self-starter.

Although these Girl Bosses follows the instructions of the team members that's apart of their child's care, these Girl Boss- Mompreneur, suits up daily, mentally, and physically like the bosses they are, as they lead themselves, their lives and the care of their children. This is the power of Girl Bosses entrepreneurs who takes the initiative and self-lead as a go-getter!
   3. Passion- Passion is one of the most important characteristics of

successful entrepreneurs.Successful entrepreneurs conduct business from a heart and spirit of passion. Passion is how they can continue working their businesses when deals doesn't go through or when they take financial hits. Their passion of why they do what they're doing, allows them to continue going forward with the mindset that believes things will get better.

Searching for solutions for my son special needs, my new found passion motivated me to create something that will allow me to solve a problem for families with unique needs (Disabilities). I wanted to give my Autistic son a greater quality of life. I didn't want to see another family,continue believing they didn't have what it takes to start a business, because of the demands of their child's care.

This kind of passion is; Leading from the heart! Passion helps you network with the right people who share similar perspectives. Passion becomes the water that drowns out the fires of doubt, the what ifs and quitting.

Four of my 10 Pillars that made me a Girl Boss, Mompreneur.

The First Pillar:
  Address Your Fears

Some of the fear's entrepreneurs' face; The fear of taking risks, rejection, change, failure, and startup costs. One of my greatest fears were believing entrepreneurship was impossible for me. These are your overworked thoughts that alters your perceptions about yourself and life. Get out of the moment, take action forward to pursue your dreams and goals.

The Second Pillar:
  Committed Self-Discipline

With committed self-discipline, you're devoted to developing the determination of doingthings to improve yourself. To effectively learn how to lead yourself and others, it requires discipline. Without committed self-discipline, you will lack perseverance in your actions, behaviors and your thoughts.

The Third Pillar:
  Intentional Mental Detox

A mental detox (mind detox) is the process of cleansing, that creates a healthy mental foundation for clarity within your mind, and thought patterns. Think about detoxing your body, this rids your body of toxins to improve better health. A mental detox is necessary, because our minds run thousands of thoughts per day. Imagine how much toxicity that's running through our mind, contributing to low self-esteem, limiting beliefs, reactive behaviors and so many other factors in our lives. This becomes roadblocks to our creativity.

Two action steps in mental detoxing:
1. Identify your negative out of control thoughts.

2. Self-reflect. This is an important pillar because self-reflection is key to self-awareness. The more we are aware of our thoughts, feelings, attitudes and emotions, the more prepared we are to stop doing things that are not serving us, and maximizing what does.

The Fourth Pillar:
Personal Development

Personal development is looking inwards as you focus on ways to better yourself. Just like parenting, becoming a business owner requires you to be the best version of yourself. When you become the best version of yourself, this impacts your personal goals, professional goals and your relationship related goals. As an entrepreneur, personal development must become an on-going process, because it builds more confidence, and you become stronger.

The first investment you must make is in yourself first. This again not only prepares you for success and achieving your goals, it also prepares you for the challenges that has the ability to thwart your success. No matter how much you know, how successful you become there is always opportunities to expand your knowledge.

Three tips that strengthens you personally, and professionally:
  1. Improve your people skills.

2. Become a consistent learner, learning new skills that are relevant to your industry.

3. Find a life coach, business coach or mentor.

*"Success is stumbling from failure to failure with no loss of enthusiasm."

We are all born with unique gifts and talents; however, some will only be discovered within life's greatest battles. The next time you face hard challenges, don't dwell on them. I challenge and encourage you to look for the hidden gifts, skills that are disguised as challenges within life's storms, as you continue learning more about yourself to experience the positive effects this can have in your personal life and in your business.

Angelina Squire

Jana Devoe

My Life as A Girl Boss

Walking in authority unconsciously was my reality for a long time. That authority was handed to me, and I received it when I accepted Jesus Christ as my Savior. I realized that what I was searching for was located and written by the inspiration of the Holy Spirit. And just to think, no good thing was being held from me-I was holding myself from my destiny as a Girl Boss.

Here in this walk of entrepreneurship; I was shown the ending and then taken to the beginning of living out the purpose of what I was called to do. All this time, I thought I was walking in my true calling, and the road shifted. Have you been there? You heard the word to go forward in faith and courage to birth out this mountain of influence or this solution to help create kingdom wealth and leave a legacy for generations to come. Have you felt the weight of this task? The ideas just kept pouring and you have to write them down so that they can be made plain.

Let's admit it- The ideas will come and flow, but you will learn that most ideas are for an appointed time. Please, please, I am pleading with you, do not try to microwave this process of God! It's imperative that you go through the process. That process is a labor of faith and love. Run your course, and please do not cut corners, as those lessons are a part of the strengthening of your life as a girl boss. You have come so far, and you can't look back on what was once just a page in your vision book, but a reality that you have moved on and you were not tenacious but daring. You must recognize that you were built for such a time as this. You were called. Provisions were steadily being made and doors were opening. Take it all in as this is just the beginning of what is in store for you as a girl boss. Ignore the distractions as each level of growth has its own challenges, but you've been weight-training and you can cast every heavy weight on the altar. Let every distraction go.

You are destined for greatness Girl Boss! What are you confessing over yourself and your business? This was one of the most important changes I had to make to my lifestyle. As a girl boss, I confessed that I was Abba's girl. I was His workmanship, and He was my exceedingly great reward! I began to love on Him as He loved on me. They were seasons where God only allowed me to discuss my plans with Him in prayer and under the direction of the Holy Spirit to share with those who were assigned to assist me with this journey of entrepreneurship.

Most often, I found myself standing strong in uncomfortable situations where my external circumstances did not disqualify me for a seat, but actually set me up for success, and allowed me to be a testament to others around me to show them that what one says is impossible-God calls possible. I had to learn to treat and acknowledge Him as my Source and He causes resources to reach me. As a girl boss, I had to walk in the strength of my feminine demeanor and stand amongst men to show them what God has called me to at that moment. I would confess that God has gone before me and has made every narrow road straight. It never failed, every obstacle that I faced to get to this hurdle brought me to a place of courage-even when I wanted to quit because it felt hard. Then I remembered how He endured the cross, and what portion of that weight I had to carry. At that moment, I remembered how those who were close to Him scattered and the crowds that once came to listen and glean from His Glory were now there to crucify Him. I recognized that I am not exempted from that same treatment.

As a girl boss, in the face of adversity, I must stand. In the face of disappointment, I must stand. In the face of drastic change, I must stand. How am I to feel? As a girl boss, I wanted to celebrate others, but I was not being celebrated. In those seasons, God was showing me that this walk can be lonely but worth it in the end. The sacrifice of being a girl boss could mean late nights, early mornings, and staycations instead of vacations. Fewer shopping trips and more business collaborations. From one girl boss to another; It's more than worth it! It's rewarding beyond anything you can imagine when you walk in the obedience of your gifting to create wealth. Go forth in knowledge and power. Always seek His face daily to ensure you are in His will and on the path. After all, He gets all the Glory!

This is just my perspective on how far I have come. When I look back on the day I said yes to this lifestyle, I can now see the growth of my mindset, giving and obedience. Oh, Girl Boss, you are going to learn obedience. This walk is not just a talk or cliché to shout or put on a t-shirt. It is truly a lifestyle. There is one final thought, please do not be afraid to get a mentor; one who can assist with your accountability. If you are a parent, like I am, you should feel the tugging to be accountable to your children. You owe it to someone to be successful.

Having a mentor is essential to your next level of living and business. Girl Boss! You can rock out revenue and recovery with a mentor. Those close to you may not understand the vision you are birthing or the reasoning behind how you now live your Girl Boss lifestyle. Just remind them that everything and everyone connected to you shall prosper. You have full free will to walk in this lifestyle and your confirmation is exponential growth, immeasurable miracle success and provision for the vision.

Life as a girl boss will have you birthing out vision after vision and nurturing the harvest. After all, you must become a good steward for all that has been given. Cast down every thought of squandering your wealth on frivolous things. Prepare for the famine and the plenty Girl Boss! You have been given this time- You Walk in It Girl Boss! Things have really come together, and you have grown, spiritually, mentally, and financially. Then God says, "Shift the very business you went through trial and fire for," you now must sell because God says He has something greater for you. How can a mighty, all-knowing God, suggest (more like command) you to release the very business you built under the unction of the Holy Spirit?

As a Girl Boss, you must discern the spirit of God, and what He is trying to get to you. Releasing a business could mean more revenue and new beginnings that could potentially be more than you could ever imagine. The difficulty of letting go of something successful, beautiful, and meaningful can be not only scary but disheartening to all that you worked hard to build. At this moment, you better trust God like never before Girl Boss! He's truly trying to get something to you. Don't miss your opportunity for growth, holding on to what was supposed to be released. God wants to test your faith-your belief system. You have to fully put your trust in God and allow Him to shower you with gifts of obedience. Think Girl Boss!

I would rather have all that God has for me instead of holding on to seasons that are changing. Don't lose your grip Girl Boss! You have everything you need to be successful. You can write out the lifestyle that you desire, but I challenge you to commit your plans to Him! Watch them flourish! Watch miracles break forth! I'm telling you Girl Boss, you have everything you need to be successful; just tap in and never tap out!

Ena Friday

My Life as a girl boss! Wow, I would have never dreamed of accomplishing a lot of the goals that were set out before me to live a better life and to show my children that no matter what obstacles you may face in life, you can do it if you keep God first. I had my share of challenges in life. I didn't have such a happy life as a child. It was not so pleasant growing up and feeling unworthy of anything great or doing something to help others was not something that was on my mind or that I set myself out to do. The challenges I faced from being a single mom, dealing with the pain of my past, and failed marriages were enough to think about. I was consumed with making ends meet and making sure my children were properly cared for as we journeyed through life.

There were so many times in my life that I thought I was able to see the light and then I would be hit with another setback. I remember the day I decided to pick up and move to Georgia for a fresh start. With my children in my mind, I felt this was going to be easy and a way to begin a new life. The first encounter was the low wages in Georgia. What most jobs were offering, I had earned almost 10 years ago. What a blow to a single mom. I was determined to make it and fight because I knew I deserved better. I always said if God laid everything out I would have to endure moving to Georgia, there was no way I would have left Michigan. God knew exactly what he was doing, but he kept his hand on me and my children through the challenges and trying times.

I felt like such a failure to my children because they didn't ask to be uprooted and moved to a new state to start life over. I felt so defeated and depressed a lot of times because the move was a lonely place; I only knew one person in Georgia. I was just trying to make a better life for myself and my children. I continued to work hard and push even when I wanted to give up. I was told that moving to a new state takes about 5 to 10 years to really see the benefits. My family and people I knew back in Michigan said I was a brave woman to be bold to move to a place where I knew no one. I said my life is dependent on this move and I am expecting some great things.

When things didn't happen as planned, I was so ashamed of the place I had me and my children in, mentally, spiritually, financially, and emotionally. I knew I had to fight harder than ever if I was going to make it in this new state with my children. I took time to focus on goals and to dig deeper within. I decided to go back to school and get my master's degree in Human Resources to add more tools to my tool belt. I worked full-time and attended school at night while raising 3 children. I would tell myself often that no one is going to give you anything; you must work hard at what you want and never give up. I always said quitting was NOT an option.

While it was tough going back to school, I became very disciplined and focused. Two years later, I graduated with honors and held a 3.8 GPA. Yay! Praises all belong to God. I was feeling so good about the accomplishment of getting my master's degree. The degree did help me land some better positions in my corporate job which has really been a blessing for me especially since I was a single parent raising 3 children pushing to make it better for my family. A takeaway I reminded myself as I was seeking to accomplish more is that you must enjoy the journey and it's a marathon, not a sprint.

While on the journey, I noticed I began to have a desire to help women, and although I didn't quite understand what that looked like, talking to women and encouraging them made me bubble up inside. I found myself hosting women in the privacy of my home having amazing conversations about life and the things we have gone through or were currently struggling with. My story and testimony would always be pulled into the conversation because some could not understand how I was able to overcome the trauma and pain I endured. I never really thought about the money part because I didn't see it as a business; I just thought I was sharing and bringing other women together to build strong relationships. It felt so nice to have other women around that could relate and desired other like-minded women to be a part of a community.

Fast forward to 2018, my gathering of women became a non-profit organization, Culinary Cakes and Conversations. Our mission was to exquisitely curate culinary events, we are committed to provide welcoming and nurturing environments that are designed to bring people together to exchange information, inspiration, and resources that support people in living lives that are healthy, vibrant, prosperous, and empowered. The feeling of moving forward in what gave me passion and a drive to support others made me realize that everything I had gone through was just for this moment and I was all for it. I gave my truth to who I was and all that I encountered and was ready to be used by God.

I remember crying out to God on many occasions after I was healed from my past hurt. I would say, "God what is my purpose? What am I here to do? How can I be sure that I am walking in it? One day, I heard, "Daughter, it will require you to be transparent, authentic and vulnerable because women all around the world needed someone to be real about their pain, trauma, setbacks and moments of giving up on yourself."

I began hosting events; women would come for my husband's amazing food and my baked desserts and were ready for what I would share. There were women of all ages; some were very mature which was shocking, but what I found was that there were women in their late 60's still hurting from childhood trauma just like the younger women. The women thanked me for being open and vulnerable and wanted more of what I had to offer. The organization is still going and right when the pandemic hit, I was on my way to finding event spaces to host events. I had become too large for my home. Because of the pandemic, I haven't hosted any events since 2019, but in 2023, we will be back in full swing with much more things to come.

During the pandemic, I focused on hearing from God, and I birthed my book," Breaking the Silence", tools for impactful conversations about the pain, perceptions, and the healing process of child sexual abuse. It was time to tell my story but to show the transformation as well as provide tools and tips for survivors, parents, children whose parents shared or discussed my book with their children and organizations of women who were dealing with survivors of child sexual abuse.

The book had women calling me and texting me saying I am ready to break the silence. I never thought anyone would do that, but they were. Some were crying, some were upset, some had many questions for me and some just were struggling but wanted to be free from the pain. I cried and cried out to God because I never thought this book would open so many conversations.

God was definitely showing me this was bigger than me; He was in it, and I said no matter what, God I am ready for more; I want to be a vessel for your women near and far. The response to the book had me seeking God for my next. I began doing speaking engagements for women in shelters, at churches, and private requested events. I knew God had me in my element and a place in my life where he would be glorified.

One thing during this stage I did realize is that I wasn't making a lot of money and there were times I paid out more than I earned. I prayed because I didn't really know what was I doing and I did have a nonprofit as well as my new business EnaNichelle Enterprises LLC where I would offer my speaking opportunities with the hopes of adding coaching and Self-Love retreats for women. I needed help. I had to invest in coaching to make sure I am earning profit as well; that is important. We don't go into business to do everything for free even if we offer free things which I have done a lot. I had to learn that this is my business and people will pay for what they need.

I am proud to say although it is taking time, it's been well worth the journey. I continue to seek ways to build my business and I am excited that I have Tia as my coach and no matter what, I will not give up on, first, God in what He has called me to do, and second, I am building a legacy for my family; something that I look forward to my daughter or granddaughters to carry on.

One of my biggest desires is to leave corporate America and be full-time business owner, hosting sell-out retreats, speaking engagements, coaching clients and building my organization. If someone asked me if this is worth it, even if my income is not where I desire it to be, would I keep going? I would say hands down absolutely. I believe in everything God has shown me and I am in the right space. I am all in. I will never give up. I am on a mission.

Princess Millens

Don't Despise Your Small Beginnings

Have you ever had the feeling that nothing was coming together for you in business? I am sure that you were extremely discouraged, right? So was I! There were several times in my life when I was always discouraged about business. I kept thinking that it wasn't working fast enough, I was not seeing results, people are not supporting me, and the list goes on. I've tried several business ideas but nothing ever panned out. I kept getting more and more discouraged because I saw great things happen for other people and nothing was seemingly coming together for me.

I tried and failed at 4 MLM companies and 3 businesses that I tried to start from ground zero and nothing was coming together. That was SEVEN businesses that I closed the door on and had nothing to show for it. I had all of these big dreams of leaving a legacy for my children, but each time coming out of it feeling like a complete failure.

I began to wonder: What was the difference between my business and my thriving friends and family? Why was nothing working out for me? As I began to reflect, I took note of something. I kept looking down on my business because it was small. Perhaps not consciously, but deep down, I viewed my business as the "lil business" thing that I was doing in hopes that it would become more than a side hustle.

After all, there have been many people whose side business became their main success, and it was no longer a hobby. But not me. I was seeing my business as small because I constantly compared myself to others' accomplishments, not realizing that we were not on the same path and did not have the same purpose in life.

When we are working on our purpose, it eliminates the temptation to compare ourselves to others. Everyone in this world has a purpose and something to do! Our paths are not the same, but it was not until I began walking in purpose that I perceived my business as growing and evolving and never small. In the past, I never included God in my business. I never genuinely asked for His help or direction. Therefore, I did not have God's heart concerning His plan for my life. Yes, we will see many people that just get rich with seemingly trivial things, but Purpose outlasts Pretending!

You must understand that small beginnings lead to big successes. No one is an overnight success. There certainly may be quick success, but we all have to start somewhere. I created a subconscious thought of perceived failure that led me to resent my small beginning. Who knows - those 7 other businesses may have worked if only I had the right mindset to accompany success. I believe that my burning desire to be successful outweighed my focus on the process of being all that I had dreamed.

Now, I'm on business numbers 8, 9, and 10 which were birthed mainly through the pain of the death of my only son, Anthony. I didn't know it then, but I was given the name of my business by God seven months prior to his death. Little did I know that it would finally be the beginning of something fulfilling and would leave a positive impact on women all over the nation.

What made the difference? I was finally walking in my purpose. Not only because of my son's passing but because of all of the experiences that I've had in my life that would greatly help someone else. Also, there had to be a mindset shift. I had to shift from thinking that any of my business was all about me. It is all about the people whom we serve! We are blessed with the opportunities to pour into other people with our products and services that will positively change their life. We are catalysts of change and nothing about us is small.

It wasn't until many years later that I began to think "What do my children think of me? Am I just an example of failure to them?" After all, this is what they saw me go through growing up. They saw business after business literally slip through my fingers into the land of the unknown, never to be seen or heard of again. I was sure that I was an embarrassment to them. My family really never knew the details of what happened with my businesses. All they saw and experienced is that I was always "busy".

Many years later, I was literally set free from the internal shame that I imprisoned myself with when my daughters began to tell me how proud they were of me! Even after the passing of my son Anthony, his friends told me that he would talk about me every day. I had no idea! All this time, I was only thinking about the businesses and feeling like a failure. However, they saw a hard-working teacher who spent 20 years doing her best to help every student in her care. They witnessed a non-degreed mother go from having only a high school diploma to a professional educator and minister with three-degree levels. And they finally saw me creating my own level and definition of success in a business that found ME.

I thank God every day for them and for reminding me that these years have not been wasted. I learned something with each one and took the lessons with me. I encourage you to never look at your past as a failure. It was a necessary part of your journey and, with the right perspective, has the power to make your next venture so much greater. So, embrace every step of the journey.

Never look at your business as small in the sense that it has no value. The word small business only relates to size, number of employees, or perhaps the amount of revenue. If you are adding value to other people's lives and helping them in areas that they would not be able to navigate without you, then you are indeed not small! I had to change my perspective about my business, and it created a turning point for my business mindset.

Through this entire process, I've learned that just because I create an LLC or file articles of incorporation, or just because I have a building, or just because I have a business license on the wall, or just because I have a fancy logo, does not make a successful business. It all begins with your mindset and is followed by your motives. Why are you in business? Is it just for money? Do you desire to help others? Your mindset will get you in the right direction, but your motives will keep you in the right direction.

Zechariah 4:10 says "Do not despise these small beginnings, for the Lord rejoices to see the work begin…". God rejoices to see our work begin! Start where you are and refrain from the toxic habit of comparing yourself to someone else. As a #GirlBoss, you must walk your own path, see your own vision, obtain your own goals, and have your own representation of success. You must have faith that it will work…THIS TIME. As an 8-time business restarter, I had to renew my faith that it would work THIS TIME. Everyone has been given something to do in the world; Learn to be great at fulfilling your purpose, even when you're small.

Father God, I thank You for every #GirlBoss business owner that is reading this right now. I ask that You give them the courage to begin again, even after a perceived failure. I pray that they receive the mindset that anything you give to us is never small. I thank You that You are Omniscient, and You know the end before the beginning of a thing. Help us to see ourselves the way Your loving, caring Eyes see Us. You have given everyone in this world something to do that shows who You are. I pray that we use our gifts and talents to give You Glory in every way. I pray for focus, clarity, and direction as You push us further in our purpose. I pray that they learn to take each experience and no longer look at them as failures, but as a chance to learn something that they need for their next level. Help us to not despise our small beginnings but remember the joy it brings You to see our work begin. I pray that You give us increased faith to work our vision through to the end and never give up. I thank You that You have made everything beautiful in its time. Great success is our portion today and always. Let Your name be praised and glorified in all that we do. In Jesus' name, and it is so, Amen.

About Our CoAuthors

As a woman of vision, Dr. Davis is revered worldwide for her leadership, integrity, and compassion. Her fiction and leadership led her to establish two ministries, FreshWinds Ministry and Widow Speaks Talk Show which can be viewed on several social platforms including ROKU TV.

Emily Wilson is a mother of three, a wife, a Mary Kay Independent Sales Director, a Virtual Assistant, an Event Planner, a Senior Clinical Data Manager and a daughter of the Almighty God! She has served as a leader for over 25 years in church and in business endeavors. She's always had a heart for people. Her ultimate goal is to leave people in a better state than they were when she first met them.

About Our CoAuthors

Tamara is a woman of God who loves empowering, motivating and inspiring women to become the women God has destined them to be. She is a wife, mother, Best Selling Author, Consumer Educator, Advocate, Master Life Coach and Entrepreneur who puts all of her faith and trust in the Lord. Tamara believes wholeheartedly that women are more than Conquerors and that with God we can do anything!

About Our CoAuthors

Melvina Pratt-Harris is a Christian Business Owner. She is wife to Joseph married almost 22 years, mother of 3, Tracy (deceased) Tarek and Imani. Grandmother of 2 Tarek Jr, Tyana and 2 bonus grands Malik and Ariyah. Her hobbies include Sewing, Journaling, and Crafting. She is a woman of many talents with a background in Nursing, Massage, Nail Tech, Childcare, the list goes on she has tagged herself as the Multipreneur. In her spare time, she is always up to something or involved in new opportunities.

About Our CoAuthors

Angelina Rideaux grew up in Austin, TX. She's 36 years old and the Founder of Rideaux's Expressions (author and inspirational speaker) as well as co-owner of J.O.T UNLIMITED ENTERPRISES LLC. She's a mother of 6 and a wife and a child of God.

About Our CoAuthors

Health/Wellness /Mindset Mastery Coach, Writer/Life Speaker, and Author, Angelina Squire. Angelina is from Miami Florida and is also the CEO of a 501 (c) 3 Non-Profit for Autism/Various Disabilities: Unique Hearts foundation Inc., giving these families a greater quality of life outside of their disabilities. Angelina's passion for Women, who are hurting from life's pain, is why she created Queens Awakening LLC where she stands as an anchor and guide, helping clients around the areas of fear, and intense difficult emotions and more. Angelina's hard life and her Autistic son, gave inspiration, helping others overcome their personal struggles.

About Our CoAuthors

Jana DeVoe is an innovative Sales & Marketing Strategist, who coaches entrepreneurs and sales trainers. She also specializes in revenue growth and organization of retreats and conferences. Most recently, Jana has added the title of author of the book "The Craft of the Follow Up. The Craft of the Follow Up is the go to guide for the entrepreneur or professional who has failed at following up with their customers, and as a result has lost numerous revenue. This guide will help as a relatable tool to get you on the right track to "stop selling" and start building" those long lasting relationships that will duplicate into sales.

Ena Friday is known as the Resilient Catalyst. The founder of the non-profit Organization Culinary Cakes and Conversations, a safe place to support and encourage living a life of freedom. The author of the book "Breaking the Silence". Ena empowers others to seek healing to live on purpose.

About Our CoAuthors

Princess Millens is the CEO of Blessed and Beautiful International offering programs and services to women who struggle with grief burnout so that they can design a plan to get their joy back and embrace their purpose. She is the mother of three wonderful children, an International speaker, a Certified Joy Restoration and Life coach, and best-selling author, and has a passionate desire to help build better families and communities.

About Our CoAuthors

Spotlight Authors

Spotlight Authors

About the Author

My Life As A #Girlboss Visionary, Coach Tia Monique is a wife, mother of six, and an ordained minister. She is also an award winning, International bestselling author, and founder/CEO of Let It Out Academy, an all inclusive writing and self publishing company.

For 5 years, she has created new bestselling authors and has assisted many authors with manuscript development, marketing, publicity, graphic design and website development. She's known for creating bestselling anthologies that feature women, giving them the opportunity to write for the first time and/or create an extra stream of income. Her clients include people from all over the United States including Gospel artist Byron Cage and Judge Mablean Ephraim.

In 2020, Tia's success and business came to an abrupt halt as she was required to undergo emergency surgery to remove necrotizing fasciitis. There, she discovered that she had tested positive for Covid-19, bringing in more challenges. Her body shut down, forcing her into a cycle of uncertainties with her life hanging by a thread.

Tia spent more than ninety days in hospitals, rehab, physical, occupational, and speech therapy. She was determined to fight back and rebuild her life and her business. Even now, in 2022, she has no use of her right hand and drop wrist on her left where she can only use her index finger to work.

"I am a poster child displaying triumph, encouraging others not to give up. If I can make it despite many limitations, they can make it too!" she proudly proclaims, "God had a plan for me because He kept me here while others died all around me. A part of His plan is for me to help others live and win."

Since making her return, Coach Tia Monique has been featured in publications on NBC, ABC, CBS, FOX, and many other regional media outlets. She is a featured speaker in a leadership speaking tour sponsored by Forbes, with world renowned speaker, Shawn Fair. She also founded The ProspHERing Women Alliance™ and The Big Business Shower™, where she's helping women follow their dreams to become proficient, profitable, and prosperous entrepreneurs.

Tia is now available to travel and take the stage to speak and motivate others, inspiring them to fight to win despite their obstacles. She is driven to help mold at least 5,000 female entrepreneurs, award-winning, bestselling authors and speakers who can use their position to eradicate poverty in their lives.

She believes that if you're free from all that's hindering you, you will be free to succeed! When you hear her speak, you'll surely hear her exclaim, "Be free to be free!™"

Connect with Coach Tia today!

You can connect with me on:
- https://www.tiamonique.com
- https://www.facebook.com/coachtiamonique

www.ingramcontent.com/pod-product-compliance
Lightning Source LLC
Chambersburg PA
CBHW050252220526
45465CB00002B/648